# The Seven Wonders
# of the Leg

*Other Books by George Whipple*

*Life Cycle* (1984) Hounslow
*Passing Through Eden* (1991) Thistledown
*Hats Off To The Sun* (1996) Ekstasis
*Carousel* (1999) Ekstasis
*Tom Thomson and Other Poems* (2000
   —Collected Poems, Volume I) Penumbra
*Origins* (2003) Guernica
*Fanfares* (2003) Ekstasis
*Footsteps On The Water* (2005) Black Moss
*The Peaceable Kingdom* (2006) Penumbra
*Kites* (2007) Ekstasis
*Swim Class* (2008) St Thomas
*The Colour of Memory* (2009
   —Collected Poems, Volume II) Penumbra

# The Seven Wonders
## of the Leg

## George Whipple

Ekstasis Editions

Published in 2010 by:
Ekstasis Editions Canada Ltd.                    Ekstasis Editions
Box 8474, Main Postal Outlet                              Box 571
Victoria BC V8W 3S1                              Banff AB T1L 1E3



**Library and Archives Canada Cataloguing in Publication**

Whipple, George, 1927-
      The seven wonders of the leg / George Whipple.

Poems.
ISBN 978-1-897430-61-3

      I. Title.

PS8595.H39S48 2010          C811'.54          C2010-903529-1

*The Seven Wonders of the Leg* has been published with the assistance of a grant from the British Columbia Arts Council administered by the Cultural Services Branch of British Columbia.

Printed and bound in Canada.

*for*
*David A. Kent and Margo Swiss*
*believers*

# Contents

## Mom and Dad



## Aurora



## Sunset

## War Memorial, 1918

# Memoir

# Memoir

At 20, saw my poems
    in a magazine; was immortal
        for a fortnight.

Settled down at 30,
    sold my head for bread,
        a servant of the city.

At 40, committed
    hari-kari for a virgin
        half my age–but survived.

Published my first book
    at 50 and discovered
        the benevolance of critics.

At 60, moved in
    with my dying father
but only hastened his departure.

Understood at 70
    if we would be immortal
        we must die.

With luck I'll pass away
    fed ice cream in a hospice
        by a former stripper.

# I'm Not the One in the Mirror

I'm not the one in the mirror,
that sagging aggregate
of temporary pleasure-dust.

I'm a halfway house, a hidey-hole,
an always refuge for the soul,
the key to every lock.

From my window seat in time
I sit and watch my resurrection.
The sun is my reflection.

Everything I see is mine.
All the wonders of the world
are where I chance to look.

And your arrival, Lord,
at my own door is me.

Private Screening

With closed eyes
   I sat and watched
      the 80-year-old
movie of my life unfold
   on the memory screen:
      scene after scene
that I had written
   made me twist
      and squirm in agony
—so few I hadn't botched.
   Yet soon as I awake
      I go daily to my desk
         in order to exist
since what I write is me
   and I can do no other.

# Being Written

I began by writing poems
in my youth.
Now everything's reversed.

I'm only a few adjectives,
a verb, a noun,
an appendage to a pencil.

I live without inhabiting myself,
not quite alive unless
I'm being written.

# The Strange One

How strange
   I must seem
      to all who know me;
at home neither in my skin
   nor in the world,
      unable to fit in,
an enigma to my parents,
   an annoyance to employers,
      a maker of wry verses,
creating something out of nothing,
   or as most would say,
      vice versa.

# Mall

I'm not the child I was
   when everything was free
      (because my parents paid)
but still it's sort of nice
   to wander through a mall
      where the God of Stuff
offers me the world—for a price.
   I like to wield my wallet's
      magic wand, create
a million factories and feed
   the starving multitudes
      —but not from charity:
however beautiful the cherry
   tree it must produce a profit
      or be chopped for firewood.

# To Be in love

To be in love
  is to share
    what you are,
to halve
  what you have;
    to be aware
that the one
  who may beguile
    you with a smile
can also kill you
  with a frown.

As animals
  flee fire
    I fled love
until I learned
  to hold it close
    without being burned
—all love's blazing
  power, glory,
    frozen in a poem
as if truly earned
  in the halidom
    and holocaust
of marriage.

# Bachelor

Standing over the sink
    I eat from a pot,
        sip my tea,
listen to the news
    made by my betters,
        the married ones
wearing suits and ties,
    who kiss their wives
        goodbye and go
to work each morning
    while I wash
        my cup and spoon,
undo my bib and wish
    them well who have
        so much to do
    undoing what
their fathers did.

# Wanderer

Sometimes at night
   I wander, stare
      through lamplit windows
at warm aquariums
   with people in them,
      and for a moment I am there
unseen within glass living rooms,
   an intruder watching
      parents reading
        by the fire,
    children spreading
  comics on the floor
—souls in suspended animation
   to me already out the door
      beneath the sharp-eyed moon,
who contemplates the stars
for more than human consolation.

# Lace Curtain

My billowing
  lace curtain, writhing
    with the wind, embraces it
    and holding tight,
  waltzes out my window
into the whirling ballroom
  of star-sprinkled night,
    a wreathing, writhing throe
of fervent exaltation—
  as I hope to leave this world,
    consumed by revelation.

# The Seven Wonders
# of the Leg

# The Seven Wonders of the Leg

Let King David
   dance with Dionysus,
      kick off his sandals,
         drop his robe and bare
            his belly to the moon,
take the Queen of Sheba
   by both eager hands
      and snakehip to
         the music of
flute playing fauns,
   piping leprechauns,
and dance the world away
   avoiding every pothole
      on the road to cha-cha Heaven,
         rejoicing in the seven
            wonders of the leg.

# Hopkins-Happy

O leafy-lively
     rah!  rah!  flowers
          cheering on the Spring,
your pink and white
     pep-rally voices
          join the voices
in my head to sing
     this Hopkins-happy
sis-boom-bah huzza!
     this boola-boola
          *rah! rah!  rah!*

# Swallows

So fast
   two seem
      as one
they arrow
   up into
      the sky
and spiral
   'round in
      figure 8s
      so near
         so far
their here
   is there
      so quick
they're back
   before they're
      gone and leave
no wingprint
   on the air…

# A Flight of Dancers

Between the seen/unseen,
  appareling the very air,
    modeling the light,
a flight of disembodied dancers
  floats into the Where
    that wasn't there
before…giving Time its toes
  and Sound a human face.
Holding hands with an arpeggio,
they clothe the emptiness of space,
as speech clothes breath with words,
  and words this act of praise.

# The Incarnation

Giant-headed
   foetus fasting
      in the airless dark,
transparent fingers
   clasped in prayer,
      no nightlight there
in the ballooning womb,
   no narcotic breast
      on which to nibble,
only a gentle sloshing,
   a slow oscillation
      when Mary moves.

## Proverbs

30

Beware of predicting the future.
No one forecast rain
but here it is
wetting the shoes
of the weatherman.

It's lonely
on top of Mount Ego.
Surrounded by ciphers
it's easy to be a legend
saluting your mirror.

I've seen graves
enclosed by fences—
to keep intruders out?
or ghosts from escaping
and stealing the women?

The stars
are calling you back
to whence you came,
the land of still waters,
of Lo and Behold.

# Some Women

Some women
  are so beautiful
    they seem to make the weather.
When it rains they must be sad.
  When the sun comes out
    it's at their pleasure.
It only snows if they wish it to,
and when fierce-eyed lightning strikes
  and storm clouds fill the air
    we know that they are mad . . .
but the most halcyon of summers
  when they let down their hair
    and consumate their love.

# When Push Is Pull



When push is pull
and go is come,
when feast is fast
and fast is slow,
when past and
future are as one
and sails uplift
the tacking moon;
when fake is fact
and funeral knell
and wedding bell
sound the same,
who does not blame
the playwright when
we fail to act?

# The Great Canadian Tradition

On my country's
  latest birthday,
    thinking of
how far we've come
  since I was young,
    and how far
we've yet to go,
  standing at
    the corner of
Despair and Love,
  I have one wish:
    let's forget
      the great
Canadian tradition
  of finding fault
    with everything
as if everything
  lacks sugar
    or lacks salt,
and spend our days
  in praise of what
    we've done
    and who we are.

# At the Unveiling

# How to Write a Poem

I

Lose yourself
in the now of noun and verb.
No arguing in pubs.
No creative writing class.
Just following your vision
like a donkey following
a carrot on a stick
always out of reach
and therefore more delicious.

II

Laureate of lovers,
a Peeping Tom on Heaven
and open as a rose
lap-dancing with the rain,
eavesdrop on the Angels,
fill a page with words,
cross out all the prose,
and there it is—the poem
hiding from all others.

# Carving

As a carving's
　　slow/swift dance
　　　　still holds
those intuitions
　　cleft by lonely Inuit
　　　　in polished stone,
I chip away the darkness
　　from all things to show
　　　　the light within.

As a glove
　　is shaped by wearing,
　　　　my soul is shaped
by each word I write
　　and bears the stretch marks
　　　　where my vision grew
but was stillborn,
　　too great for any
　　　　language.

# At the Unveiling
<br>
*for Gwendolyn MacEwen and Al Purdy*


Banned from Toronto's pristine
parks for reading poetry out loud
and defying the police
sent to restore the Sabbath peace,
two lovers of the spoken word
have opportunely died
and been reborn as monuments inside
those very venues and are graciously allowed
to stay as long as they are only seen,
not heard.

# On Not Meeting Margaret Avison



I remember
not meeting Margaret Avison
in her Mustard Seed dim lair
sitting small and straight
in a wooden straight
backed chair
her hair
in a tight
grey tidy bun
typing, tap-tap-tap,
on some work of charity.

I had come
to that upper room
to show my work but was
too shy to enter there
and slunk away before
she was aware
that a wuss
had stood a moment
by the open door
of that little room,
her second home.

# On Woodland Paths

Unhallowed now,
   Nature has become
      a gym for joggers,
trails for mountain bikes,
   toilets for dog walkers
      gathering dog dung.

No one glimpses dryads
   ghosting through the trees
      or notes the naiads
bathing in the rain
   or reads the poems
      written on the leaves.

Poets now
   pcrform in pubs
      for the delight of donkeys
who hee-haw at the gross
   and guffaw at the loss
      of faith in everything.

# P. K. Page

Let's not forget
that aristocrat of craft,
high priestess to us all who wrap
words around the inarticulate—
her eyes like a raven's
bright and ravenous
for the white diamonds in the caverns
of her kitten-whimsical, metaphysical
sharp mind where she mined her intricate
carved gems unequalled by her johnny-one-note peers.

On the mountain top of 90 years
she began to disintegrate
and woke, as she predicted, dead,
but living still wherever that great
Grande Dame of letters shall be read.

# Emily Carr

Stopping her crude caravan
in the heart of a magic wood
she wrote in her journal:
*God, what have I seen,*
*where have I been?*
*Something has spoken to*
*the very soul of me.*
And setting up her easel,
she called ecstatic trees
into existence on an evergreen
tranced canvas, watched by Woo
her pet monkey in a sailor hat.

# Fortune Cookies

Baking what I know into a few
fortune cookie sophistries
before the oven cools
and the bakeshop closes,
I remember my imaginary friend
and how we used to hide
behind the chesterfield, delighting
in each word the other said
without the impulse, need,
to put everything in writing,
fill the cookie jar of Time
with images that tease the taste
of those who savour what they read.

# One-to-One



I remember
    that first apple blossom
        union with the world
when no snowflake fell
    in the wrong place,
        when I was freed
            from two-ness,
        made one-to-one
with stars and moon,
    on speaking terms
        with animals and birds,
an adolescent Adam
    amid all the newness.
        Or like a Noah
sailing an imaginary ark,
    the rainbow's arc
        my guide at dawn,
the lantern fish at night,
    and mermaids swimming
        all around me singing.

# Stradivarius

The Stradivarius
that no one plays
is only catgut,
bits of glued
frustrated wood.

The path
that no one walks
turns to weeds
as the poem no one reads
does not exist.

# Studio

Within this word-room, smithy, cave,
I court the lightning, breed my books.
What does it matter if they're read
or not:  I had the joy of their begetting.
Do wheat sheaves in shaved meadows care
if, ground to grain, they're baked in bread?

In paper boats I launch my words
to cruise the rainy gutters of the world
and when they're gone, I'll go into the light,
help Monet paint the rainbows, watch
my parents rise from crematory ash,
and asking their forgiveness, bask in their reply.

# The Language Tree in Winter

Lord, let me not connive
at my own death.

Grant me one last blessing, give
me a few poems still to write
and by their writing let me live
although half dead, still half alive.

On the great green tree of language
let me bear that winter fruit
which only a Death dodger can produce
by sorrow pruned and ripened by the years.

# Mom and Dad

## Mothers

What of her from whom I came,
quarried from cut flesh
that bled me on my way
with no reward but a sometime smile,
who taught me my first prayers
and in death still hears
me cry from that long ago child's crib
and struggles to get up and see what's wrong.

And what of our foremother
who, precocious from the sea,
first ventured out onto the shore
where everything was new and frightening—
all her dreams fulfilled at last in us
walking on hind legs and breathing air.

# Before My Mother Was

Before my mother was I was;
   before I left the sanctum
      of her chosen womb
         I knew her name.

I saw her working
   in New Brunswick for
      an old photographer,
         tinting tintypes
   with a tiny brush,
turning grey skies blue,
   brown shadows green,
making the pale features
   of his clients blush.

I saw her walk beside
   me as I rode a donkey 'round
      the ring at Sunnyside
         when I was two.

Day and night I watched
   as year by growing year
      she made four walls a home
         and made the four walls sing,
became the happy atmosphere
   in which I breathed and moved,
   was nourished, clothed and loved
just for choosing her as mother—
each one giving birth to the other.

# Ten Thousand Suppers

My mother baked
  and cooked all afternoon
    from her secret recipes
  our ten thousand suppers
until dad and I came home to sit
  around the kitchen table, blest
    by the fragrant and best
food that we would ever know
  garnished by her dimpling wit
    and with laughter for dessert.

# Your Other Mother

As snowflakes gradually erase
  the shape of things below,
    life imperceptibly wears
      intellect and body down
until dying in the room where you were born
  you see a shadow standing at the door
    —the woman who will give you birth
in your next attempt at meriting
  admittance to that snowless place
    where the sun shines evermore,
and where there are no calendars,
  no need of writing books
    to make yourself immortal.

# The Long Green Ladder

55

Sea nymphs
    wearing seaweed saris
        in some coral grotto
            fathoms deep,
watched over my amoeba
    through slumbering long eons
        till the destined time
when I was old enough to climb
    the long green ladder
        reaching to my father
shaving by the kitchen sink.

# Bluffer

My father
  had my number,
    called me Bluffer;
knew I thought
  that I was not
    his only son
but someone who
  had wings that flew
    me far, far away
—unlike the other
  kids who were
    their fathers
as their fathers
  were *their* fathers,
    from generation
unto generation—
  deep buried roots
    with no imagination.

# Dad

All your life
you only smiled
when I disappointed you
whose only pleasure
was reading the daily news
and the apostles.

All your life you waited
for me to grow up
but I never did
until you died,
leaving me at 55
to marvel at
how wise you were.

# When I Left

When I left
what was once my father
turned to ice,
my thoughts
turned into clouds
white as that face
where no tomorrow was.

Taking off the costume
of the flesh, he closed
the door on space and time
and walked into the light,
that anathema to those
who won't take Yes
for an answer.

# Aurora

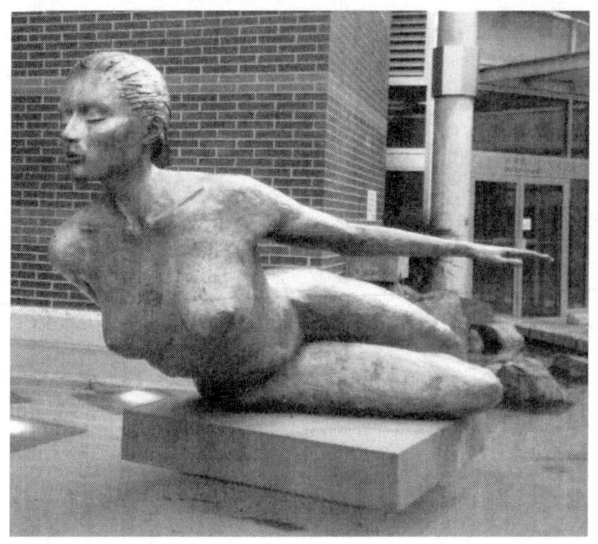

# Aurora

Leaping mountains,
    sprinting through
        green valleys,
blushing the pale cheeks
    of virgin lakes,
        embracing farms
and villages, she chases
    shadows through the streets
of the tall omnipotent
    stone cities—lounges
on the topmost parapets
    of glass-glistening
        gold towers,
puts her healing arms
    around the crowds below
        and calmly moving on,
leaving her warm
    footprints everywhere,
takes evening by the hand
    and slowly disappears
        across the sea.

# The Sun



The sun
   seems most happy here
      walking slowly through
       this garden, lighting
the scented candles of the flowers.
  Here everything is mute
    like the chicken tracks
      of a poem in Chinese
which, alas, we cannot hear—
unlike the silence where
    Elijah heard Jehovah.

# Storefront

Looking long and long
at this aging storefront
I feel the love,
the brotherly affection
that we share as comrades,
survivors of the Hungry '30s.

Stucco broken off,
paint peeling in the sun,
door hanging by one hinge,
I share the beauty, riches
of falling to pieces,
becoming pure Being,
the way we were
before the builders came
or my mother was.

Gastown

Historic squares;
    brickwork alleys,
        quaint boutiques
selling English lavender,
    tea cozies—souvenirs
        of the long ago
colonial lost years—
    grenadiers in garrisons,
        cobbled streets,
clip-clopping horses
    drawing open carriages,
        a world of British
prudence, dignity and peace
    broken by wild cries
        of "Gold! Gold!
            We're *rich*!"

# Northern Star

A chopper
  blinks across
    the pre-dawn dark
telling traffic how to pare
  a minute from point A to B
    while out in interstellar
      space the Northern star
which saw the Earth's creation,
  the change from ape to Man
    on an African savannah,
invention of the wheel,
  Roman chariot and SUV,
    looks down impassively
on cars that crawl like ants
  around a cantaloupe.

# Hotel Lobby

The homesickness of luggage
dropped off somewhere between
where the heart is
and the rest of the body.

Old World paintings no one sees.
A grand piano no one plays.
Grandiose bouquets on great
baronial oak tables.

A place of robots
handing out tagged keys
to indifferent rooms
that smell of desolation.

## Eyes Sullied

Eyes sullied
  by looking
    without seeing;
ears dulled
  by too much noise,
    I came upon a place
that happifies the blind
  with sweet music,
    and closed captions
      for the deaf—
  where caterpillars,
    doing push-ups
cross a cabbage leaf,
  and the wind
    whispers in my ear
'Let majestic man
  like an ocean liner
    cruise the sea-lanes
of the world, the ship
  was made by woman
    and runs on woman power.'
Though poets kiss the moon
  and give a bit of tongue,
    their love lies more
      in the intention
  than the consummation
like the suitcase
  no one claims
    going 'round and 'round
  the carousel when
everyone has gone.

# Half a Man

Lying on his back,
  stunned, stupified,
    watching shadows shift
and lengthen on the ceiling
  of his rented room,
    guts twisted,
      heart constricted,
        loins aflame,
obsessing on the girl
  he met last month
    or last week
    or only yesterday,
he understands at last
  that he is lost—
    only half a man,
and thinks of marriage,
  making money, kids,
    whose only care
had been his beat-up car,
  nights at the local bar,
    weekends playing poker.

# Some Days Make You Weep

Days that stink of mouldy wood,
days when fog lifts her skirt
only to her ankles
revealing just the lower
floor of forty story buildings;
days even elephants forget,
days an ancient turtle
which belonged to Cleopatra
wants to close its eyes and die,
days we no longer remember the sun,
days with no fast forward or rewind.

# Rocks

70

Shattered boulders;
  broken rocks
    at the foot
of earthquake-
    battered mountains—
      these will retain
        a memory of us
in scattered scree,
  cromlechs, cairns,
mute megaliths, menhirs,
  when we have fled
    this black planet
      for a greener one.

# Sunset

# The Light of Evening

The most
  precious light
    of day is the light
of evening, the valedictory glow
  on redbrick tenements
    like the cry
      of the castrato
  lamenting the loss
of his manhood,
  or like the sigh
    of a bridesmaid
      at the wedding
of her rival.

# Sunset

74

A sunset seen by thousands
is a thousand sunsets
but only one of them is yours.

As we climb out of this world
each day's a handrail clutched
more tightly as the years advance,
and even ice is warm to those
whose hands are colder.

What present life's more precious
than the one we left?  The womb
of time has windows ... I've looked
both in and out.

                When crows
divebomb a squirrel between
two sanctuary elms, I remember
Armageddon as if it were tomorrow.

# Church Steps



Although church steps outwear
   the soles of rich and poor
     and are scuffed hollow
in their turn, I still believe
   that there is nothing more
     than the chancel roof
between me and eternal life.
   Although grave Science says
     there isn't any proof
and all the world shouts No,
   I know what I know.

# God Is in the Silence

St Francis said
    to preach without
        the use of words.
And very few
    when talking to
        animals and birds
and to their lice.

God is in the silence—
    as Christmas lights
        are more luminous
when reflected on
    a  polished floor
        where cedar-scents
of cinnamon and spice
    aromatize the eyes.

The spirit listens
    without ears
and from the windows
    of the body stares
        through cyberspace
where time dissolves
        into Eternity.

# Each Day I Lose

Each day I lose
a little more,
see a little less
although I try
to look faster.

So little time
to look around the world
before the eye-gates close,
trying to discover
what only the dead know.

So many unwanted births!
So many foolish deaths,
unless someone is steering
the raft on which we float
downriver in the dark.

# Vasectomy



I think of those
living inside out,
who wish to be forgotten,
their Gregorian, grieved voices
rising as if from the grave
on behalf of a lost world
—novitiates on skinned knees
giving up their lives down here
for better ones above
as a vasectomy returns
saved sperm back to the donor.

# The Assizes of Heaven

79

Where comets flash
  and shooting stars
    punctuate the dark,
no one handcuffs God
  or accuses him of lying;
    no appellate court
calls Jonah to the stand
  or dares indict the sun
    for stopping on command,
or Judas for complying
  with the resurrection
    as someone had to do.

# Before There Was Prozac

Before there was Prozac
   there was religion,
     solemn ceremonials
   that seem ridiculous
to those who think that God
   is just a knot of neurons
     in some corner of the brain
       more easily aroused
   by an electric probe
than by prayer.

So science ends
   where faith begins
     its leap toward the Source—
as salmon leap, fall back
   and leap again—again—against
     the torrential force
       of common sense
to where knowledge ends
   in wisdom, the real
     in the more Real.

# Agog for Marvels

Agog for marvels,
  between the Real
    we can't recall
      and the False
    we can't forget,
we look for revelation
  beneath a magnifying glass
    or within the reach
  of strong telescopes—
two worlds beyond belief
  revealed by man's research
    but not by Providence
—as poems are which start,
  not as a piece of paper,
    a pencil and a moving hand
      arranging words
into a pleasing order,
  but as a synthesis
    of soul and body,
      sound and sense
  crossing the border
between Real and False
  as an optical illusion is
    both one thing and another.

# The Mystic

*If I think, everything is lost.*
Paul Cézanne


When the sixth sense
   illuminates the other five,
      I do not think, therefore I am.
Faring without feet, I walk the world
   and know what stones are saying.

The doubting eye lays waste
   the inner landscape of the soul
      as at the confluence of daffodils
         and traffic, monoxide drowns
   the scent of flowers.

Why google God when he is everywhere?
   Dream awake; paint with your eyes;
      speak without words.  And without hands,
go gather that invisible red rose
   known only to the blind

who see the chirping of small children
   as a kaleidoscope of colours,
      hear the autumn odours
of raked and burning leaves as fugues
   where all six senses join.

All accidents epiphanies,
   I have visions without shape, am oned
      with weather-beaten driftwood
         silvered of the moon
   on Arctic beaches.

# War Memorial, 1918

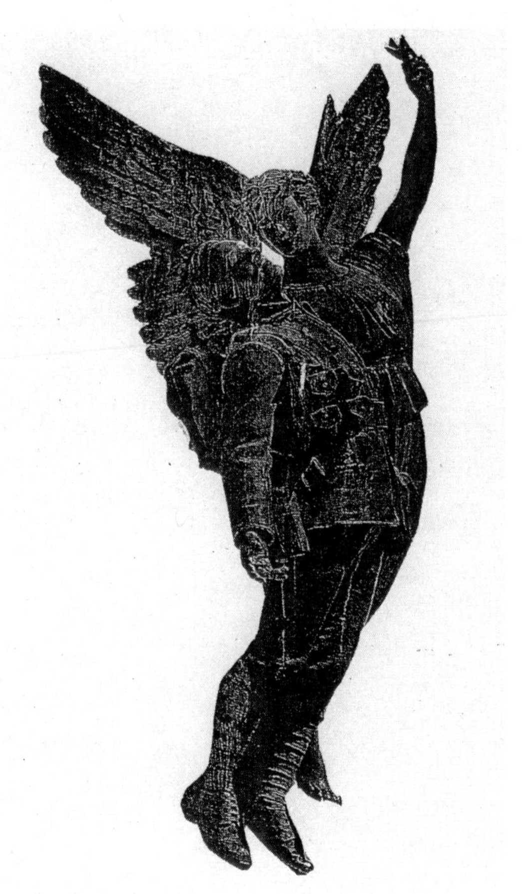

# Back Story

As windows presuppose a wall,
  Paradise a snake
    and matter anti-matter,
is our world only a faint echo
  of a Big Bang, a firework
    set off for a joke?

Do we die when we die
  or are we the back story
    to an amazing sequel,
  as my father's wife
    is my mother,
and all mothers Eve?

My childhood was more wise
  than Solomon because
    I had no thought of death,
    no need of faith . . .
I had my omnipotent blue blankie,
  my teddy bear called Mabel.

# Headstones

Their whole life a hyphen
between a birth-date
and the date of death,
the old lie buried
in full flower
along with those who died
with all their seeds intact,
children with their hands
still sticky from the caramel
in a box of *Cracker Jack*,
who raced across the road,
noticing too late, too late,
the car out of control.

# Russ Maywood

As cemetery earth
  slowly heals around
    your granite scar;
as paintings leave
  a gallery wall to live
    on in the memory,
I think of you, my jocular
  Beau Brummell friend.

As magnetic trees
  draw covens of black crows
    like iron filings
      to their boughs,
I follow in the footsteps
  of the rain to where you lie
    and wait the rainbow's
  coat of many colours.

# The Book of Earth

What written masterpiece
  is more symbolic
    than the Book of Earth—
      repentant trees
with bowed heads
  still mourning
    their forced labour
      at that execution
        long ago—
and flowers in their rainbow
  and salvific glory
    rising every April
from the kingdom of the dead
  to corroborate the story
    too great for any pen.

# War Memorial, 1918

In full battle dress, upborne
on the right arm of his bronze
repatriating Angel
(her left hand
brandishing the wreath
he won by rushing to his death
with no arduous adieus), he soars
above shell-shattered no man's land
into Vancouver heaven.

# Runes

Expect nothing.
Take counsel of the wind,
patience from a stone.

Sow the seed you're given.
Take pleasure in the planting,
leave the harvest to another.

Life is not retroactive.
The fallen leaf
does not return to the tree.

Remember the thin ice
that lured you farther out,
then opened up behind you

as you fled to shore,
one step ahead of drowning.

# As a Hanky

As a hanky
   in breast pocket
      fortells a sneeze;
as crossed fingers
   portend lies,
and heavy eyelids
   coming sleep—
      so failing heart
   and slowing blood
evoke my agile soul
   growing stronger
      day by day, getting
   ready to outleap
its body bag.

# Misers of Misery

Misers of misery (whose appetite
can only be appeased by that apple pie
with neither cinnamon nor apples),
we cat-and-mouse with evil, blame
the crisscross patterns on our palms
or adversary stars when we do wrong.

Hormones drive the wise man mad,
make the strongman weep,
drive the most virtuous of women
to drown their children, leap
into the dark abyss
of a lover's arms.

Misers of misery, we hiss
and spit at the morning sun
who spreads his glory everywhere,
makes the common housefly
sparkle like an amethyst
and sprinkles gold dust
through a glass of applejack,
and in the cut glass facets
of a crystal bowl.

# Pain

Pain can be a sickness,
a failed love affair,
an accidental wound.

Like death, it's an escape
from time—there is only pain
with no before or after.

Both pain and pleasure
come from God knows where
like poems or the weather.

# *You*



When you are old
  everyone reminds
    you of someone else,
there are no new faces.
  There is nothing you
    haven't seen before,
nothing you haven't heard
  and yet you go on looking
for the square without corners,
  the music more than sound,
joy greater than all pleasure,
  until hopefully you hear
    Love ask, *Who are you?*
and you softly answer, *You.*

# Paradise

I think of those
    who are nothing,
        who lie in their own filth
          at the end of alleys
zonked out on plonk or crack,
    who have no need of bodies,
        eyes swollen shut
          on a paradise
of beautiful young maidens
    bringing them clean needles
        where wine pours down like rain
and the best uncut cocaine
    is laid out for the taking
        while the cops are kicking
            them awake to face
                the street again.

# Will There Be Children

Will there be
   children by your bed
      when you pass on,
and lit candles in all
   the great cathedrals
      in memory of you,
         and will the pontiff
            speak your eulogy
where you lie so neatly dressed,
   so photogenic in your coffin;
      and will there be
a long, slow, sad cortege
   of black limousines
      following your hearse
         to a marble crypt,
and hundreds standing in the rain
   with raised umbrellas
      mourning your departure;
and will your absence
   be any the more absent
      than the pauper's
         being buried
in an unmarked corner grave,
   your darkness any the less dark,
      your light any the more bright
         that leads you both above
to where you had your start,
   and everyone's related,
      having the same Father?